I am a
SIKH

I am a
SIKH

Manju Aggarwal
meets
Harjeet Singh Lal

Photography: Chris Fairclough

Religious Consultant: Bhai Bhagwant Singh

W
FRANKLIN WATTS
LONDON•SYDNEY

Harjeet Singh Lal is nine years old.
His family are Sikhs. His father,
Mohan Singh Lal, works in an
electronics factory near their home in
Southall, West London. His mother,
Ravinder Kaur Lal works as a
machinist. Harjeet's brother Randeep
is eleven. His sister Gurpreet is
twelve and Inderjeet, his other sister,
is seventeen.

Contents

© 1984 Franklin Watts
This edition 2001

Franklin Watts
96 Leonard Street
London EC2A 4XD

Franklin Watts Australia
56 O'Riordan Street
Alexandria, Sydney, NSW 2015

ISBN 0 7496 4177 0

Text Editor: Brenda Clarke
Design: Peter Benoist
Illustration: Tony Payne

Printed in Hong Kong

The publishers would like to thank
the Lal family and all other people
shown in this book.

10 9 8 7 6 5 4 3 2 1

Going to the Gurudwara

Sikhs can pray to God at any time. Even so, I go with my family each week to the Gurudwara, to worship with other Sikhs.

The Gurudwara is a Sikh temple, or shrine. Its name comes from two words – Guru and Dwara – which mean "the place of the Guru". A Guru is a teacher. Many Gurudwaras fly a yellow flag in the shape of a triangle. The flag is called Nishan Sahib and shows that this is a holy place for Sikhs.

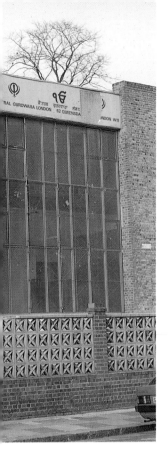

Before we go into the temple we take off our shoes. They stay in the porch until we are ready to go home.

Sikhs enter the temple in bare feet as a mark of respect. Inside the Gurudwara, which is a large hall, men and women can worship together. The head is kept covered as a mark of respect to the Guru Granth Sahib the Holy Book. This is usually on a platform so that it can be seen from all corners of the hall. Men usually sit on the floor on the right and women on the left.

Worship and prayer

We go to the Gurudwara for Sangat, which is prayer. First I kneel before Guru Granth Sahib, the Holy Book. I bow and touch my forehead on the floor. Then I sit down on the carpet.

The Holy Book is covered in a fine, bright cloth and rests on a cushion beneath a canopy. The Book is at the centre of worship. Small offerings of money are made to The Book.

The service begins with Kirtan, the singing of hymns from the Holy Book.

The singing is accompanied by music from tabla and harmonium. Recitations are then made from the Holy Book and the priest – the Granthi – explains the scripture. At the end of the service everyone stands with hands folded while the priest recites the prayers. Then a sacrament called Prasad is given out. It is made from flour, butter and sugar.

The Holy Book

My father helps me to understand the teachings and script of Guru Granth Sahib, the Holy Book.

Guru Granth Sahib was compiled by Guru Arjan, the fifth Sikh Guru. He completed it in 1604. He used a script, or way of writing letters, which was established some 60 years earlier by Guru Angad, the second Guru. The script was called Gurumukhi, "from the mouth of the Guru". This is the script that Harjeet is learning to read.

10

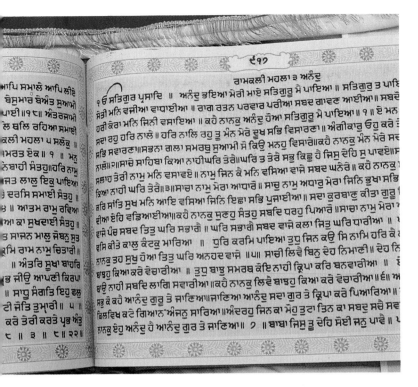

The Sikh script

U	A	I	S
ੳ	ਅ	ੲ	ਸ
H	K	KH	G
ਹ	ਕ	ਖ	ਗ
GH	Ṅ	C	CH
ਘ	ਙ	ਚ	ਛ
J	JH	Ñ	Ṭ
ਜ	ਝ	ਞ	ਟ
ṬH	Ḍ	ḌH	Ṇ
ਠ	ਡ	ਢ	ਣ
T	TH	D	DH
ਤ	ਥ	ਦ	ਧ
N	P	PH	B
ਨ	ਪ	ਫ	ਬ
BH	M	Y	R
ਭ	ਮ	ਯ	ਰ
L	V (W)	Ṛ	SH
ਲ	ਵ	ੜ	ਸ਼
KH̤	G̤	Z	F
ਖ਼	ਗ਼	ਜ਼	ਫ਼

On some evenings I go to the Gurudwara school to learn more about the Gurumukhi script. After lessons I say my prayers.

Sikhs believe there is only One True God. The Gurus were great teachers who laid emphasis on faith in God, and the importance of good conduct and a happy society. Vices like smoking for example are forbidden. The Holy Book teaches about God and Creation, and about Man and his place in the universe and how man can seek enlightenment and salvation.

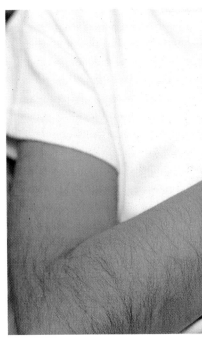

The five symbols

My father explains to me the meaning of the five Sikh symbols.

The strict Sikh must wear the five symbols all the time. Each one begins with the letter K – Kara, Kangha, Kacchehra, Kirpan and Kesh and Keski. These symbols were introduced by Guru Gobind Singh, the tenth and last Guru, to denote the Sikhs as the Khalsa – the pure. Nowadays, not all Sikhs wear all five symbols and some even cut their hair.

On my wrist I am wearing one of the symbols, the Kara or bangle.

The Kara is the sign of eternity and is made of steel. Kangha, the comb, is a symbol of cleanliness. It keeps the hair knot in place. Kacchehra, the pair of shorts, is the symbol of action and goodness. Kirpan, the sword, is a sign of strength. The fifth symbol is Kesh and Keski – the hair and turban. The emblem of the Sikhs is the khanda – a double-edged sword, circle and two scimitars.

13

Putting on a turban

The turban – Keski – is the symbol of wisdom and is very important to Sikhs. It is an insult to try to remove somebody's turban.

Sikh men do not shave their beards or cut their hair. For comfort and safety they wear a cloth turban over their long hair. They comb the hair into a bun and hold it in place with a cloth called Patka. A band – fifti – is tied on and knotted at the back. Then the turban is wound all round.

I need my father's help to tie my turban as the cloth is 2 metres long. My father's turban is made from cloth over 4.5 metres long.

The turban cloth, starched to keep its shape, is folded lengthways. About 15 cm is draped over the left shoulder and the rest is wrapped round the head from right to left. The end of the cloth is tucked into the forehead and the piece on the left shoulder is tucked in at the back.

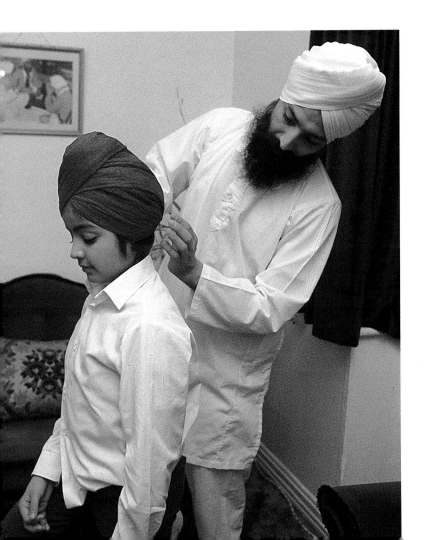

Sikh clothes

We are going to a wedding soon. Inderjeet bought a new suit, but my mother made one for Gurpreet. I went with her to buy the material.

Sikh women sometimes wear the long dress called a sari. But most wear the Punjabi suit, or salwar kameez. The long scarf called a dupatta or a chunni – is used to cover the head as a mark of respect in the Gurudwara and also in the presence of older or respected people.

I do not have to wear traditional clothes either at home or at the Gurudwara, but my father changes into Punjabi clothes before prayer when he comes home from work.

Most men in their daily life wear European clothes, but the turban is always worn. However at religious ceremonies many men wear Punjabi clothes. The Granthi, our priest, is wearing these – a white turban, white long shirt and white trousers.

The history of Harjeet's family

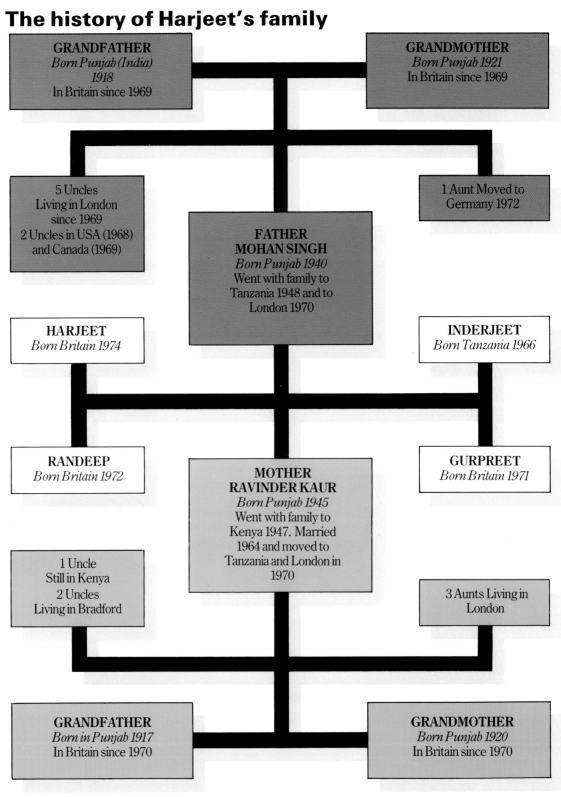

GRANDFATHER
Born Punjab (India) 1918
In Britain since 1969

GRANDMOTHER
Born Punjab 1921
In Britain since 1969

5 Uncles
Living in London
since 1969
2 Uncles in USA (1968)
and Canada (1969)

1 Aunt Moved to
Germany 1972

**FATHER
MOHAN SINGH**
Born Punjab 1940
Went with family to
Tanzania 1948 and to
London 1970

HARJEET
Born Britain 1974

INDERJEET
Born Tanzania 1966

RANDEEP
Born Britain 1972

GURPREET
Born Britain 1971

**MOTHER
RAVINDER KAUR**
Born Punjab 1945
Went with family to
Kenya 1947. Married
1964 and moved to
Tanzania and London in
1970

1 Uncle
Still in Kenya
2 Uncles
Living in Bradford

3 Aunts Living in
London

GRANDFATHER
Born in Punjab 1917
In Britain since 1970

GRANDMOTHER
Born Punjab 1920
In Britain since 1970

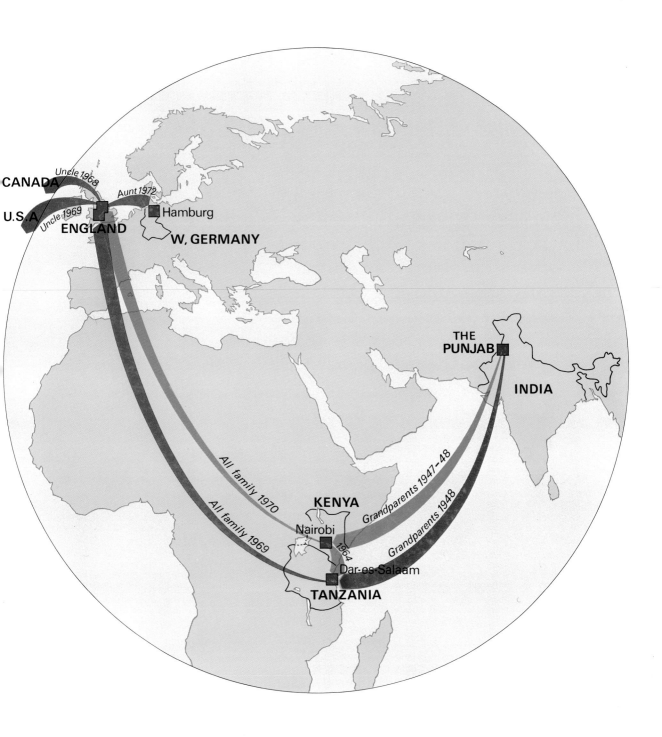

CANADA

Uncle 1968

U.S.A

Uncle 1969

ENGLAND

Aunt 1972

Hamburg

W, GERMANY

**THE
PUNJAB**

INDIA

All family 1970

KENYA

Grandparents 1947-48

All family 1969

Nairobi

Grandparents 1948

1964

Dar-es-Salaam

TANZANIA

Eating the Sikh way

My family is vegetarian. We do not eat meat as we think it is wrong to kill animals for food. But not all Sikhs are vegetarian.

When a ceremony is held in the Gurudwara, men and women help to prepare the food. This food is prepared in the community kitchen called the Langar. It is always vegetarian, usually vegetable curries and chapatis. Food is served to all who wish to eat. Everybody sits on the floor to enjoy the meal together.

Some of my favourite foods are gulabjaman, a sweet made from milk. Another is rasgulas, made from curd cheese dipped in syrup.

Harjeet's mother prepares meals for the family at home. Sometimes he helps with the shopping. Some foods can be bought ready-made at the grocer's. Harjeet likes samosas, a sort of pancake filled with vegetables and fried in hot oil. He also buys pakora, a dish of spiced vegetables fried in batter.

The importance of music

Randeep and I are learning to play drums. The instrument is called a tabla. One of my sisters plays the harmonium and sings. The other sister plays the sitar, which is something like a guitar.

Music has an important place in Sikh life. It is played at home, in the Gurudwara and at other gatherings. Only the tabla and the harmonium are played in the Gurudwara as a rule. The harmonium is a keyboard instrument.

I enjoy seeing and listening to the expert musicians who play in the Gurudwara.

Music is played at all the important religious festivals and musicians are treated with great respect. Singing plays a major part in the ceremonies at the Gurudwara, where musicians sing verses from Guru Granth Sahib. They also explain the meaning in song. At times the congregation joins in the responses.

A Sikh Wedding

The wedding we looked forward to was my uncle's. He and my aunt sat together in front of the Holy Book. My aunt wore Punjabi wedding clothes.

Before the couple married, the families of both the man and woman had to agree to the match. Both young people also had to agree. At the ceremony, the bride was given the bridegroom's sash by her father. This signifies the giving away of the bride by the father to the bridegroom.

All the families at the wedding gave money to the bride and bridegroom. My uncle carried his gifts at the end of the cloth.

At Sikh weddings, four verses of Guru Granth Sahib are read out. This reading is called Lawan. Then the bridegroom leads the bride slowly round the Holy Book, once for each verse. The priest who has read the verses leads the ceremony. Money is always given as a wedding present and the bride's family prepares the wedding feast.

The ten Gurus

I have to learn about the lives and teachings of the ten Gurus on which the Sikh faith is based.

The ten Gurus are shown above. The first was Guru Nanak (top middle), who founded the Sikh religion. He was followed by other Gurus who added to the ideas and customs of the religion. The last was Guru Gobind Singh (bottom middle). He said after his death the Holy Book should become the Guru for Sikhs. Guru Gobind Singh is also seen opposite.

We remember the lives and works of Gurus in festivals each year. A special one is called Baisakhi.

Baisakhi is celebrated on 13 April. It is begun with a ceremony called Akhand Path when the Holy Book is uncovered. Verses are then recited. On this day in 1699 Guru Gobind Singh formed the Sikh brotherhood – the Khalsa. Baisakhi is also seen as the first day of the Sikh year.

The Sikh Year

Sikhs use the Hindu lunar calendar which means that the months start with each new moon. All festivals, apart from Baisakhi, have different dates each year. They are called Guru Purab – holidays associated with the Gurus.

DECEMBER
MAGAR
NOVEMBER
KATIK
OCTOBER
ASUN
SEPTEMBER
BHADRO
AUGUST
SAWAN
JULY
AR

MARTYRDOM OF TEGH BAHADUR
Poh – 1 day
The Guru was tortured and then beheaded by a Mogul Emperor in 1675. He refused to convert to Islam. Hymns and readings in the Gurudwara.

BIRTH OF GURU NANAK
Katik – 1 day
The most holy festival. He was the first Guru. Celebrated by a full reading of the Holy Book finishing on the morning of the festival. The whole day is then spent in the Gurudwara singing hymns, listening to poetry and stories. Lunch and snacks are prepared and eaten there.

DIWALI
Katik – 1 day
Celebrates the release of Guru Har Gobind from prison. The Gurudwara is lit up and there are fireworks. It is also a Hindu festival day – known as the Festival of Lights.

The text around the circular calendar reads (clockwise): JANUARY, MAGH, FEBRUARY, PHAGAN, MARCH, CHAIT, APRIL, VASAKH, MAY, JAITH, JUNE, OH

BIRTH OF GURU GOBIND SINGH
Magh – 1 day
Celebration of the life and works of this very important Guru. Hymns are sung, readings made from the Holy Book and food eaten in the Gurudwara.

HOLA MOHALLA
Phagan – 1 day
Celebrates the day set by Guru Gobind Singh to show Sikh military power. In India, his home town of Anandpur is the main festival centre.

BAISAKHI
Vasakh – 1 day
The birthday of the Khalsa founded by Guru Gobind Singh in 1699. A continuous recitation of the Holy Book is begun 48 hours before the festival. In India the festival begins the harvest – also seen as the first day of the New Year.

MARTYRDOM OF GURU ARJAN
Jaith – 1 day
The Guru who compiled the Holy Book was tortured to death by the Mogul Emperor in 1606.

Sikh Facts and Figures

In 1971 there were about 10.4 million Sikhs in India – about 1.9% of the population.

Sikhs have emigrated to many countries of the world since Indian independence in 1947. The places in which Sikh communities are found include Britain, East Africa, Canada, the United States, Malaysia and most European countries.

In Britain there are thought to be about 250,000 Sikhs – the largest number in any one country outside India.

The Sikh religion was begun in the Punjab in north-west India by **Guru Nanak** (1469–1539). He was born a Hindu. The nine Gurus who followed Guru Nanak were:

Guru Angad (1504–1552) He began the use of Panjabi in Sikh ceremonies rather than the Hindu sanskrit.

Guru Amar Das (1479–1552) Taught the importance of living a good life and of service to others.

Guru Ram Das (1534–1581) Founded the town of Amritsar where the Golden Temple was later built.

Guru Arjan (1563–1606) Compiler of the Holy Book, Guru Granth Sahib.

Guru Har Gobind (1595–1644) A great military leader and religious teacher.

Guru Har Rai (1630–1661) Taught the need to do good to others and not cause pain or harm.

Guru Har Krishan (1656–1664) The youngest Guru – he died at the age of eight.

Guru Tegh Bahadur (1621–1675) Preferred death to changing his religion to Islam.

Guru Gobind Singh (1666–1708) Formed the Brotherhood of Sikhs – the Khalsa – and named the Holy Book as the last Guru and teacher of the Sikhs.

Sikhs live according to certain rules laid down by the ten Gurus. These include:
– belief in one God who created the universe.
– the need to earn an honest living and share with others.
– not using alcohol, tobacco or drugs.
– rejection of the Hindu caste system of high and low people.

Glossary

Baisakhi A festival which begins the Sikh year.

Chapatis A kind of round, flat bread made out of wheat flour.

Fifti A band of cloth used in tying the turban.

Granthi The holy priest.

Guru The Panjabi word for teacher.

Gurudwara The Sikh temple; meaning the place of the Guru.

Guru Granth Sahib The Holy Book containing the sacred writings of the Sikhs.

Gurumukhi The script in which the Panjabi of the Sikhs is written – the original script used for the sacred writings of the Sikhs.

Guru Purab Holidays associated with Gurus.

Kacchehra A pair of shorts.

Kameez A long shirt or tunic.

Kangha A comb.

Kara A bangle (steel bracelet).

Kaur The name given to all females initiated into the Sikh community – means "Princess".

Kesh Hair.

Keski Turban.

Khalsa The Sikh order of Brotherhood. The word is said by Sikhs to mean "Pure" or "God's Own".

Kirpan A sword (dagger) worn by Sikhs.

Kirtan The community singing of hymns.

Nishan Sahib The Sikh flag.

Patka A cloth used to secure the hair.

Salwar Trousers gathered in at the ankle, worn with a tunic.

Sangat The Sikh congregation assembled for worship.

Singh The name given to all male members of the Sikh Khalsa – means "lion".

Sitar A stringed musical instrument.

Tabla A pair of small drums.

Index